I0901206

HELP!

DISABILITY PRESSURES OUR MARRIAGE

Ernie Baker

Consulting Editor: Dr. Paul Tautges

Help! Disability Pressures Our Marriage

© 2019 Ernie Baker

ISBN
Paper: 978-1-63342-155-4
epub: 978-1-63342-156-1
Kindle: 978-1-63342-157-8

Published by **Shepherd Press**
P.O. Box 24
Wapwallopen, PA 18660

www.shepherdpress.com

All Scripture quotations are from the ESV.

All rights reserved.

No part of this publication may be reproduced, or stored in a retrieval system, or transmitted, in any form or by any means, mechanical, electronic, photocopying, recording or otherwise, without the prior permission of Shepherd Press.

Designed by **documen**

Contents

Introduction

Changes in life can come about unexpectedly, and these changes often bring pressure with them. This is certainly true in the world of disability. Maybe you were shocked by news that your newborn, or soon-to-be-born child, had a disability. Or perhaps you were hit with the news that your spouse's injury was going to have permanent consequences. Maybe your "new normal" has become so consuming that you are beginning to realize that something else is suffering as well: your marriage.

Perhaps you picked up this little book because you feel that so much attention has been concentrated on the physical care associated with disability that you and your spouse are not as close as you used to be. You have been increasingly irritable with each other, or worse, maybe angry fights have erupted. It could be that one of you is even considering leaving the marriage because this is not how you envisioned your life.

Do any of the following describe your marriage?

- » Financial pressures seem overwhelming.
- » You feel ignored by your husband or wife.
- » There's little or no time for your sexual relationship. Maybe it's no longer even a possibility, due to new physical limitations.
- » Disagreements about how to discipline your child with disabilities, or your other children, arise frequently.
- » You are exhausted and discouraged by the unending care that disability requires.

These realities raise some important questions. Is it possible to have a close and healthy marriage, now that caring for your spouse or child with a disability has become the focus of life? Is it possible for your marriage even to improve due to the disability? The answer to both questions is "yes." But how is this possible?

Marital joy, success, and stability are all possible because there is Someone who makes a difference. This is incredibly good news! A relationship with Jesus Christ makes healthy relationships possible, even in the midst of intense pressure. In other words, since Jesus is the Preeminent One, he can change or stabilize the climate in your home if you walk with him by faith.

Essentially, that is what this mini-book is about. Therefore, my purpose is threefold: to take an honest look at how disability pressures marriage, to examine the deepest desires of the heart which such pressures often reveal, and to provide hope by showing how the Lord provides strength and help through his always-relevant Word.

1 Unexpected and Intense Pressure

As a pastor, I am privileged to shepherd many couples whose marriages are being pressured and changed by disability. Since disability enters families in myriad ways, it's impossible to address any one way in specific detail. However, perhaps you can relate to elements in one or more of the following real-life stories.

John and Amanda woke up one morning not knowing that in a few hours their lives would change forever. It was impossible for them to foresee John having the accident which severed his spinal cord and left him paralyzed. This change immediately placed significant financial burdens upon them, creating many related pressures. Their house needed major alterations to make it wheelchair accessible, and they also needed a vehicle upgrade. In particular, however, these changes impacted their marriage. In one conversation which remains vivid in my mind, Amanda agonized and, in tears, revealed to me one of her fears: "What we've had [referring to their physical intimacy] will never be the same again."

Tony and Jo thought life was wonderful when they brought Rhonda home from the hospital. She was a beautiful baby and looked perfectly healthy. However, they soon began to wonder if something might be wrong. Jo describes those days:

> *Rhonda looked so normal lying there amongst the toys and other paraphernalia of a newborn's room. But I soon realized that every time I would check on her, she would be in exactly the same position I had originally put her in. . . .*
>
> *Many nights during those first months, I would get out of bed and stand over Rhonda's crib praying that she would wake up and begin crying and demanding attention. She would rarely cry. When she did there were never any tears. She never cried when she wanted to be fed or have her diaper changed. Nothing about her development was normal.*[1]

Little did Tony and Jo realize the pressures that the needs of their precious little girl would bring into their marriage.

Jane, a fellow-pastor's wife of twenty-five years, had major intestinal surgery just three years into marriage. Life has never been the same since she had her colostomy. Now, when they sleep, she has to have IVs drip liquids into her body, since her digestive system can barely absorb fluid. Part of my friend's daily routine is now caring for his wife.

When they stood at the marriage altar, none of these couples knew what was to come. None of them knew they would either become 24/7 caregivers or needing that care themselves—but God did. For all of them, their marriage vows, "For better, for worse, in sickness and in health, till death do us part," have taken on new, pointed, realistic meaning.

Common Concerns

While writing this mini-book, I interviewed several couples. Marriage already has enough stress even when disability is not present, but it was easy for me to see how tense things can get when additional pressures are added. Here are some of the common concerns I heard.

Disagreement over Child-Discipline Issues

Andrew and Rachel's son was born with two special conditions: he is blind and he has a rare skin condition. When I asked them what the biggest strain on their marriage was, they replied,

> *It's been deciding the best way to discipline our son. As much as we try to work together and be firm in our discipline decisions, we often compromise and use the excuse that he cannot see.*

Rachel said she tends to let things go because she feels sorry for him because he has a disability. She added,

> *This has led to arguments between Andrew and me because now Jayden is being allowed to get away with things he really should not be doing. It is very easy to [impede] a child with special needs and let him or her run the parents and make their own rules.*[2]

Maybe, like Rachel and Andrew, you and your spouse do not see eye-to-eye on how firm to be with your child who has a disability. Perhaps the discipline of your other children is being neglected because the care associated with your child who has a disability is so consuming.

Irritability and Lack of Physical Intimacy

Other couples confessed that it is easy to be irritable with their other children and with each other because of how time-consuming the care of their disabled child has become. Along with this are sexual pressures and, in general, a lack of intimacy. One husband told me he regularly feels ignored by his wife because the needs of their child are so demanding upon her. His wife is often so tired that their physical intimacy has suffered. Though he understands that their child's needs must be met, the feelings of loneliness are real.

Financial Pressures

Added to this is the pressure of money being scarce. Doctors' and hospital bills keep coming in the mail, and insurance companies constantly send paperwork. Keeping up with the insurance forms can seem like a full-time job!

Many ask, "Why does there have to be so much pressure?" But the deeper question is, "What is the source of all the pressure and suffering in the world?" We will answer those questions in the next chapter.

2 Good News from God

As a pastor and counselor, I regularly help those who are suffering from the impact of life circumstances. But have you ever wondered where all of this brokenness comes from? Why does there have to be so much suffering in the world?

The Source of Pain and Suffering

The Bible tells us that human suffering originates in the events recorded in Genesis 3. But to understand this, we need to go back a bit further.

Everything God Made Was Good

In Genesis 1–2 we read how God made this world beautiful and perfect. Following his creation, at the end of the sixth day of creation week, God pronounced everything "very good" (Genesis 1:31). There was no suffering, no pain, and no death.

Adam and Eve, the first human beings, were part of this "very good" creation. We, too, are each created by God. We are designed to live in relationship with him. Every human being is an "image-bearer" of God (Genesis 1:26–27). Additionally, the Bible teaches that we are completely dependent upon God:

> *In him we live and move and have our being.*
> (Acts 17:28)

> *The earth is the* Lord*'s and the fullness thereof,*
> *the world and those who dwell therein,*
> *for he has founded it upon the seas and*
> *established it upon the rivers.*
> (Psalm 24:1–2)

Since God is our Creator, we are accountable to him, and therefore will answer to him one day.

If everything God made was originally good, what went wrong?

A Fallen World

When God created the world and placed human beings in it, he established standards for them to uphold. He gave Adam and Eve a simple, clear command:

> *You may surely eat of every tree of the garden, but of the tree of the knowledge of*

good and evil you shall not eat, for in the day that you eat of it you shall surely die.
(Genesis 2:16–17)

Sadly, they did not obey. Instead, they rebelled against God's good laws, and the whole human race fell into sin (Romans 5:12). Instead of believing that their Creator had their best interests in mind, and cherishing the beautiful freedom he had given them to eat of every tree of the garden except one, they trusted themselves and disobeyed him. They took the forbidden fruit and ate it (Genesis 3). By not trusting the Lord, they demonstrated that they did not love him.

Their sin had devastating consequences, not only for their souls, but for their bodies as well. Their bodies started to decay; the ground produced thorns; and the thorns produced pain. It has been this way ever since.

As another consequence of this sin, there was immediately pressure on family relationships. The first relationships experienced divisions as Adam blamed Eve (and God) for the problem (Genesis 3:12). Then, in the very next chapter, we read of how a brother slaughtered his own brother (Genesis 4)!

Our Lost Condition

Since Adam and Eve's fall all human beings have been lost. We are determined to figure out life on our own, but we make wrong decisions. We are guilty of violating God's standards by living for our own. But Scripture is clear that

> *None is righteous, no, not one.*
>
> *(Romans 3:10)*

Because God is the King of the universe, it is treasonous to go against his wishes. There is a penalty for doing so:

> *The wages of sin is death.*
>
> *(Romans 6:23)*

Elsewhere, the apostle Paul removes our blinders and bluntly describes us in our sinful state as

> *foolish, disobedient, led astray, slaves to various passions and pleasures, passing our days in malice and envy, hated by others and hating one another.*
>
> *(Titus 3:3)*

But it is even worse than just violating God's standards. Because we were made to be in relationship with God, and it was to be a loving, trusting relationship, sin is about our seeking satisfaction elsewhere. The prophet Jeremiah says that humans have a tendency to drink from the wrong fountain:

> *Be appalled, O heavens, at this;*
> *be shocked, be utterly desolate,*
> *declares the* LORD,
> *for my people have committed two evils:*
> *they have forsaken me,*
> *the fountain of living waters,*
> *and hewed out cisterns for themselves,*
> *broken cisterns that can hold no water.*
> (Jeremiah 2:12–13)

It is like an adulterous relationship. In marriage, you are to be satisfied with each other's love. When adultery happens, the sinning spouse is seeking satisfaction elsewhere.

The situation is truly bleak. Our sin-nature does damage to our relationship both with our Creator and with others. We turn inward, and self-focus poisons our lives from the inside out. We become blind to the reality of relationship with the Creator.

A Perfect Savior

Into this hopeless scene rides a majestic warrior to do battle against our enemy of sin and to provide the solution to our severed relationship with God, and power to overcome our stubborn desires. Jesus pierces this blinding darkness with brilliant light, declaring,

> *I am the light of the world.*
>
> (John 8:12)

In Jesus, we have a Savior—one who can relate to our experience of weakness. He understands pain. Hundreds of years before Jesus was born in Bethlehem, the Old Testament prophet Isaiah prophetically described the physical and mental suffering that would mark Jesus's earthly life:

> *His appearance was so marred, beyond human semblance,*
> *and his form beyond that of the children of mankind . . .*
> *He had no form or majesty that we should look at him,*
> *and no beauty that we should desire him.*
> *He was despised and rejected by men,*
> *a man of sorrows and acquainted with grief . . .*

> *Surely he has borne our griefs*
> *and carried our sorrows . . .*
> *But he was pierced for our transgressions;*
> *he was crushed for our iniquities.*
>
> (Isaiah 52:14; 53:2–5)

Jesus's body was beaten and bent over on the cross as he suffered the weight of judgment on our sins. We can be forgiven because he paid the debt for our sin we owed to a holy God. Paul must have relished giving this good news:

> *But when the goodness and loving kindness of God our Savior appeared, he saved us, not because of works done by us in righteousness, but according to his own mercy, by the washing of regeneration and renewal of the Holy Spirit, whom he poured out on us richly through Jesus Christ our Savior, so that being justified by his grace we might become heirs according to the hope of eternal life.*
>
> (Titus 3:4–7)

Jesus can relate to your suffering; he himself is very familiar with sorrow and grief. He was rejected by the men and women he had created.

He can relate to disability. If you feel weak, battered, and bruised by life, he knows how you feel. As the suffering Savior, he is the one we can go to whenever we need help:

> *For we do not have a high priest who is unable to sympathize with our weaknesses. . . . Let us then with confidence draw near to the throne of grace, that we may receive mercy and find grace to help in time of need.*
>
> (Hebrews 4:15–16)

Are you trying to bear the challenges of disability alone, or are you going to the Savior for help? He cares, but how are you going to know he cares unless you are communicating with him? This means you must have a relationship with him.

Switching Loyalty

Before hearing the good news about Jesus Christ, the apostle Paul's spiritual confidence was in his own good works and loyalty to his religion. But once he understood that Jesus had died in his place, paying the just penalty for his, Paul's, sin, and had been raised from the dead, Paul turned from faith in himself to faith in Christ. This was the moment of his conversion (Acts 9 describes this in detail).

His is one of the clearest testimonies in the New Testament of switching from a previous way of life to becoming a follower of Jesus. In Philippians 3 he writes,

> *If anyone else thinks he has reason for confidence in the flesh, I have more.*
>
> (3:4)

He then lists his former loyalties. As a Pharisee, Paul was loyal to Judaism—to the point of persecuting others. He was loyal to his family heritage. He was loyal to his education in the law and to living by it. Then something miraculous happened: he experienced the light! His blinded eyes were opened, and he switched loyalties. Now he could say,

> *But whatever gain I had, I counted as loss for the sake of Christ. Indeed, I count everything as loss because of the surpassing worth of knowing Christ Jesus my Lord. For his sake I have suffered the loss of all things and count them as rubbish, in order that I may gain Christ and be found in him, not having a righteousness of my own . . .*
>
> (Philippians 3:7–9)

What are you loyal to? What are you hoping for? What is your confidence in? Instead of trying to find hope in the "broken cisterns" the world wants and your heart craves, there is something—Someone—better! Turn from them and to him, the Preeminent One. You can even do that right now.

Tony and Jo Knott have powerfully testified that knowing the Lord has kept them stable. They write,

> *We cannot imagine how a family could survive the many trials, heartaches and valleys of raising a disabled child without Jesus at the center of their marriage.*[3]

So what is the solution to all our pain and the curse of sin on our world? It is a person, Jesus Christ, who himself suffered intensely and overcame. Although he died on the cross, he rose again and ascended into heaven, where he is now the Exalted One. He understands your pain, but also wants to make his power available to make relationships healthier for those who trust in him. He is able to do this for you, even if your marriage is under pressure because of disability—and it is to this we turn in the next chapter.

3 Encouragement in the Midst of Pressure

The sufficiency of Christ to meet all our needs is wonderfully portrayed in the New Testament book of Colossians, and in this chapter we will draw encouragement from this book written by the apostle Paul. My yearning is that you will gain hope as you see how Jesus can stabilize your marriage when you follow him.

The Intense Pressure

The background to the book of Colossians is suffering of the most intense kind.

Relational Tension

One of these forms of pressure is slavery. It is hard for us to imagine what life for a slave in Roman times was like, but a man named Onesimus knew. I mention his name because there is a logical connection between Colossians and another smaller Bible book, Philemon, embedded in which is the story of the runaway slave Onesimus—a story of betrayal and the need for forgiveness and restoration.[4]

Onesimus had run away from his master, Philemon. But through meeting the apostle Paul he became a follower of the Lord, upon which Paul sent him back to Philemon. Paul urged Philemon to forgive Onesimus and welcome him back.

The connection between this background and the book of Colossians explains why Paul speaks about relationship issues so thoroughly in Colossians (see 3:5–17). He is concerned that the gospel make a difference in the way Christians relate to one another. Scripture deals with the reality of pressure in relationships. For some of those to whom Paul wrote, it was the pressure slavery added to their relationships. For you, it may be disability.

Maybe disability has made you want to run away just as Onesimus did. Or could it be that you are like Philemon and need to forgive your spouse because of the tensions you are feeling in your relationship?

False Views of Life

Another immense pressure for the believers Paul was writing to was the false views of life others were trying to impose upon them. A group of teachers were telling them that, while they did need Jesus, he was not enough: they also needed to keep the Old Testament law in order to be saved from sin. To counter this erroneous teaching, Paul emphasizes the sufficiency and majesty of Jesus,

> *in whom are hidden all the treasures of wisdom and knowledge. I say this in order that no one may delude you with plausible arguments. . . . See to it that no one takes you captive by philosophy and empty deceit, according to human tradition.*
>
> (2:3–4, 8; see also 2:10)

Can you relate to feeling the pressure of wrong teaching? Maybe there are people who are putting pressure on you by saying that if you had more faith, your child or spouse would be healed. You may already be feeling guilty that your child or spouse has physical difficulties; should you be feeling guilty for not having enough faith as well? But this would be like saying, "God is withholding good and punishing your child/spouse because of your weakness." What a horrible view of the Lord!

Maybe you have faced the wrong philosophy of a doctor wanting you to abort your baby when you found out there was a disability. This added even more pressure to an already tense and fragile situation.

Imprisonment

To top it off, Paul, the writer of Colossians, was in prison. In 1:24 he talks about his "sufferings," and in 4:10 he refers to a co-worker as "my fellow prisoner." Paul knew what it was like to suffer. It would be horrible hypocrisy if he thought it was all right for him to tell others to be patient and put up with each other (3:12–13) but then gave himself an excuse for being irritable, demanding, and harsh.

Be honest: Have you ever felt like you are in prison in your situation? When you feel trapped by your situation, how do you respond to your spouse?

Paul, and the people he wrote to, understood pressure. But Paul believed that the Lord and the power of the gospel would make a difference in suffering lives. Why was this?

Who Is Jesus in the Pressure?

Jesus himself stepped into a pressure-filled and anxious world. He who is God became a man, walked into broken lives, and himself became broken. Here is how Paul portrays Jesus to the Colossians:

- Jesus is the all-powerful Creator but also a sufferer (1:16–17, 20).
- Jesus is infinitely holy, but he invites us, those who are defiled by sin, into a tangible relationship with him (1:18–20).
- Jesus is perfectly just, but he lavishly forgives (1:14).
- Our goal is to be made be like Jesus, and this is possible through our being "in him" (2:10).
- Jesus is the one who died but who is now alive (1:18).
- Jesus holds the universe together (1:17) and teaches us how to hold relationships together, giving us the power to do so (3:1–3).

Paul wrote all of this to people living with intense pressure, like you.

If we are trusting in Jesus as our Savior, the One who is all of these things and more dwells in us, and this makes it possible for us to have Christlike relationships—as amazing as that sounds!

If Jesus can hold the universe together, he can certainly hold your marriage together. You may say, "But you don't know how bad it is"—to which I would urge you to remember how big Jesus is. Remember also that he was raised from the dead. You have the Resurrected One on your side. If he has power over literal death, he can certainly raise your dead marriage. If he can forgive you for your offenses against a holy God, he can certainly help you forgive your spouse. If he can be patient with you, he can certainly give you the motivation to be gracious with your spouse. He is preeminent, supreme, and on your side.

This is what happens when we come into relationship with him. Because the gospel is not just a message to believe but a person to follow, when we become followers of Jesus, his Spirit unleashes his power in us to change us. He wants to change us totally, but, in particular, he is interested in changing the way we do relationships. The book of Colossians makes this very clear. Since we are "in" Christ, he develops his character in us. We enter into relationship with others who are also "in him" and in whom he is developing his character. Jesus does not fight himself!

The wonderful news is that relationship with the Supreme One, Jesus Christ, makes healthy relationships with others possible, and this is true even in the midst of intense pressure like disability. It is possible because he surpasses all others, and makes his power available to us when we are united to him through the gospel.

The Atmosphere of Relationships

The pressure from disability can do a tremendous amount of damage to a relationship. When you are tired and exhausted, if you are irritable and short-tempered, it builds walls between you and your spouse. It is easy to retreat into yourself and think, "I must get through this on my own"; "I just have to work harder and be tougher." This is the opposite of what the Lord desires: he wants you and your spouse to be loving teammates walking through life together. But how does this happen? Colossians teaches that it is through developing our Lord's character traits in relationship to others. These traits can create a wonderful climate in your home, and we look at them in detail below.

However, we need meaningful motivations for working on these character traits. One of the motivations Paul gives in this letter is that we have come into relationship with the Creator of the universe through his grace. He describes us as "chosen," "holy," and "beloved" (Colossians 3:12). We deserved to pay the penalty for our sin, but our gracious God intervened and paid for it himself on our behalf. We are rebels and should be forever alienated from him, but he has chosen us and drawn us close as those who are loved. He puts us "in Christ" so we can be considered holy.

Think of yourself as a dirty child in a rundown, filthy orphanage. The living conditions are so bad that you have open sores and skin rashes. One day, a couple come and, even though they see your horrible condition, they choose you! You are then taken home, cleaned up, and loved. Over time, your sores heal, and you grow and mature into your new identity as a member of their family. If you are a Christian, this is something like what the Lord did for you.

If you have this type of attitude toward your spouse, your home can have a beautiful Christlike atmosphere even as you live with the pressures of disability. This is possible through being in relationship with the Supreme One and learning his character traits.

Eight Character Traits to Develop[5]

When I engage in marriage counseling, I often say to the couple, "Good marriages do not just happen, they are made to happen." In other words, relationships require investment. What qualities should you invest in to make your relationship beautiful? We find the answer in Colossians 3:12–14:

> *Put on then, as God's chosen ones, holy and beloved, compassionate hearts, kindness, humility, meekness, and patience, bearing with one another and, if one has a complaint against another, forgiving each other; as the Lord has forgiven you, so you also must forgive. And above all these put on love, which binds everything together in perfect harmony.*

Here the apostle exhorts us to put our faith into action by "putting on" eight Christlike character traits which should govern our relationship with one another, even when that relationship is under intense pressure.

Compassion

Paul tells us that we need to be tenderhearted toward one another, just as God has been toward us. Matthew uses this word "compassion" to describe Jesus's response to the crowds:

> *When he saw the crowds, he had compassion*

> *for them, because they were harassed and helpless, like sheep without a shepherd.*
> (Matthew 9:36)

Jesus was deeply moved by the needs of the people in a distressing situation. Are you compassionate toward your spouse? Or is the opposite true?

The opposite of compassion is hardness, maybe showing condemnation instead of mercy, or being aloof, uncaring, rather than merciful. Do you see what this might do to your relationship? The situation you find yourselves in is already hard enough; do not make it worse by withdrawing from your spouse and becoming hardened toward him or her.

It often helps me to be tender toward others if I ask myself how I would like to be treated if I were in a similar situation (see Matthew 7:12).

Kindness

Next, Paul presents kindness, and this is how God relates to us in salvation. We deserved wrath for our sin, but he was kind instead. Paul elsewhere talks of "the immeasurable riches of [God's] grace in kindness toward us in Christ Jesus" (Ephesians 2:7).

The opposite of kindness is harshness, maybe

even meanness. What would you say is the climate of your home—kindness or harshness? If it is harshness, what is your responsibility in changing it? On the other hand, what could you do to show kindness?

Humility

Our Lord was lowly of mind. Instead of standing up for his rights, he was willing to be humbled. This word "humility," however, captures more than humble actions; it is a disposition of putting others first. In Philippians 2, Paul describes Jesus' humility beautifully:

> *Though he was in the form of God, [Jesus] did not count equality with God a thing to be grasped, but emptied himself, by taking the form of a servant . . .*
>
> (2:6–7)

In the verse directly before this, Paul instructs us to "have this mind among yourselves, which is yours in Christ Jesus" (2:5).

These characteristics define the spirit of a home. Will you be someone who stands up for his or her rights, or are you willing to put yourself second? If you are willing, because of your relationship with the Lord, to be a compassionate, kind servant, your marriage will be more stable because of you. Consider this: it is hard to fight with this type of person!

Is there a difficult task related to the care of your child or family member that you could carry out to show your desire to follow the Lord's example of humble servanthood?

Gentleness

The original word in Greek that Paul uses here is sometimes translated "meekness" and is another characteristic of Jesus. The God of the universe was meek and gentle: what an amazing thought! Paul underlines this in 2 Corinthians 10:1 when he entreats his readers "by the meekness and gentleness of Christ."

The opposite of this beautiful character trait is an aggressive, domineering loudness that suppresses others, or unbridled strength. Are there ways this is coming out in your home?

Consider this: When are you most tempted toward lack of gentleness? What could you do to respond differently?

Patience

Next, Paul urges his readers to be long-suffering with each other. It should take a lot for them to get angry. Peter says that, "God's patience waited" in the time of Noah (1 Peter 3:20). Being short-tempered, impatient, and irritable sets up a fear-filled atmosphere. If you are like that, it is not safe for others to talk to you. Often, they will withdraw through self-protection. It is impossible to have a healthy home that is withstanding the pressures of disability if those are the attitudes and actions being displayed. What can you do so that this changes?

Bearing with One Another

I am so thankful that the Lord puts up with me! He bears with us all in the midst of our weakness. The opposite attitude to this is seen in many of the things we have noted above.

On what issue(s) do you need to show more tolerance to your family members, whether or not they have a disability, bearing in mind the struggles they are also experiencing?

Forgiveness

This forgiveness is unconditional, undeserved, abundant grace such as we have received from the Lord. Forgiveness should flow like a gushing river out of our relationship with Christ, given how much he has forgiven us.

The opposite of an attitude of forgiveness is toxic for relationships. Being resentful, dwelling on the offenses of others, and wishing them harm destroys closeness.

The command here is explicit. If you have any complaint, forgive, even though the person has not earned it. Just as you received undeserved favor, so grant it now to others.

You may say, "But you don't know the extent of the offense," "I just can't let it go and give forgiveness," or, "That's not fair." When my soul whispers (or yells!) these things to me, I reflect on the following:

» I remember how much I have sinned against God (see also Matthew 18:21–35). I have probably committed the same offense against the Lord of the universe. If he can forgive me in Christ, I can forgive others in Christ.

» God keeps the record books and is a God of justice. He, the Judge of the universe, will make all things right. No one is going to get away with anything unless they repent. I must let the all-wise God handle the offense so my soul can be relieved of the burden.

How about making a decision right now, based upon how much you have been forgiven, to forgive your spouse for whatever way you believe you have been sinned against?

Above All, Love

Christian love for one another flows right out of relationship with Christ. It is a sacrificial love that seeks to put the needs of others first (see Philippians 2:3–5). In fact, Paul claims that this one character trait will hold everything together (Colossians 3:14).

The opposite of this love is so destructive to relationships! Self-centeredness that is motivated by self-protection and putting your own needs first causes harm.

Is there something you could do, related to the care of your child or spouse, that would demonstrate this type of love?

These eight character traits, from the right motives and from the right source (Christ), will hold any marriage together. Jesus can make a difference, but you must surrender your life, your situation, and your marriage to him! How about putting this mini-book down and doing that right now?

But please also consider the opposites to these

positive character traits; they create an atmosphere in a home that makes it more like a Category 5 hurricane than the peaceful atmosphere of the Prince of Peace. Of course, some tension is inevitable because we live with other fallen people and in the midst of fallen circumstances.

What kind of climate are you creating in your home? Are you an easy or a hard person to live with? Are you a high- or low-maintenance husband or wife? Life is hard enough, so I don't want to be hard to live with.

4

How Jesus Brings Hope to Our Relationships

It is easy to blame your spouse, those around you, or the circumstances for your bad response to your situation. This is the typical human thing to do. But while those things can contribute to the problem, Scripture says that our responses to pressure ultimately reveal our own hearts. Allowing our hearts to control us and our responses to others will bleed away a relationship of hope. We need the Lord to change our hearts' desires so that we respond differently to pressure; then hope can be restored.

Our Lord makes it very clear that the way we talk to others is related to the "treasure" of our hearts. He said to the Pharisees,

> *You brood of vipers! How can you speak good, when you are evil? For out of the abundance of the heart the mouth speaks. The good person out of his good treasure*

brings forth good, and the evil person out of his evil treasure brings forth evil.
(Matthew 12:34–35)

Maybe, when feeling tension in relationships, your tendency is to clam up. Just as Jesus said, "Out of the abundance of the heart the mouth speaks," so we could also say, "Out of the abundance of the heart the mouth does not speak."

Do you see the direct connection between the mouth and the heart? Did you notice how, in verse 35, Jesus used the word "treasure" in place of "heart"? That will be significant later.

What Is the Heart?

In the Bible, the "heart" means your inner immaterial person that is made up of your thought life, your emotions, and your will. This means that your thought life reveals your heart. Your decisions (your will) reveal your heart. And your emotions tell you about your heart. This becomes even more important if we take seriously Proverbs 4:23:

Keep your heart with all vigilance,
for from it flow the springs of life.

It is clear that the heart influences all we do—and that includes how we handle conflict.

Hebrews 4:12 tells us that our hearts have "thoughts and intentions." This verse underlines the "thought life" and "will" aspects of our definition. If it is true that your heart is your mind, emotions, and will, you ought prayerfully to see if you can discern patterns in your thinking, decision-making, and emotions during conflict that reveal what is truly going on in your heart. In other words, your thought life tells you where your heart really is during conflict; your decisions reveal the true focus of your heart (for example, do you decide to avoid people you are upset with?); and your emotions are a vivid picture of what's happening on the inside (for example, are you afraid of what the other person might say if you raise your concerns?).

Since my "heart" also signifies my "intentions," my "will," it makes sense to say that there are things my heart is wanting. I think about the things I want, I make decisions related to the things I want, and my emotions are especially strong when I don't get the things I want. Another word for "wants" is "desires." We are wanting, desiring beings.

It's All about Worship

The word "worship" comes from an Old English word that literally means "worth-ship."[6] It would be accurate to say, then, that what I ascribe worth to is what I worship. What am I serving? What do I love? What do I talk about? What am I willing to sacrifice for?

We saw above that Jesus used the word "treasure" in conjunction with the word "heart" in Matthew 12. My inner person is described as my "heart" but also as my "treasure." How can you tell when someone is treasuring something? Wouldn't the list of questions to ask be the same as those listed in the previous paragraph?

This is all tied to the idea of worship and the heart. The Lord wants to be Lord over my mind, will, and emotions; because of the gospel, he is transforming my mind, will, and emotions to be like his. This Lordship starts in my heart (mind, will, emotions), and the heart is the place of my treasures. So what do your thinking, decision-making, and emotions reveal about who or what is truly lord of your life? What are you treasuring?

Our lives are to be lived as one continuous act of worship; whatever we do, we are to do all to the glory of God (1 Corinthians 10:31). The Lord is to be the One we primarily desire to serve, are devoted to, bow down to, show love toward, talk about, and sacrifice for. He is to be our greatest Treasure.

Changing the Focus of Your Heart

Perhaps by this point you realize that your heart is in the wrong place. But there's hope: you can change! I frequently tell counselees and people I'm training, "If false worship is the problem, true worship is the solution." In other words, figure out what the opposite of the false worship is and start to practice that; true worship will then overcome and replace the false worship (sometimes quickly, but most often over time).

Let's take three common heart themes that feed conflict: living for the approval of others, desiring to be in control, and loving comfort.

Pleasing People: Treasuring the Opinions of Others over the Lord's

During times of conflict, people-pleasers are afraid to speak, or will say things just to please others. They are consumed with worry over what others are thinking. The kind of thought that goes through their minds is, "What will they think of me if I say what I really believe?" Rather than talking, they may clam up.

Controlling Others: Desiring Others to Do What You Want Them to Do

The thought lives of control freaks are often dominated by how to get others to do what they would like them to do. Such a person may even joke, "If only others would follow my ideas, the world would run much more smoothly!" These people get upset when their plans are not followed or others don't seem to respect their opinions as much as they think they should. Life could seem "out of control." Their communications with others are taken as orders. The tone of voice they use may be harsh.

Loving Comfort: Treasuring Relaxation and a Hassle-Free Life over the Realism That Life Has Pressure because of a Fallen World

Those who struggle with this type of heart theme usually see relational tension as a major hassle because they just want life to be fun and relaxing. They might think about those they are in conflict with, "Why can't he/she just relax and not make such a big deal out of things?"

Each of these heart themes reveals false worship because something is treasured above the Lord. They are not the responses of a person who is worshiping the one true living God.

Many things could be said concerning how to combat each of these heart problems, but first we must see that they all have a common theme: they have a low view of the LORD.[7] The people-pleaser is more concerned about what others think than about what his or her Lord thinks. The control freak can become obsessed with keeping life under control, forgetting that there is a sovereign LORD over all the earth whom we are to trust. The comfort-lover has a small view of life; if this person could get a bigger view of what his or her life is about before the Lord, that person wouldn't be as consumed with taking it easy.

Replacing Disordered Worship

The way to combat all three problems is to worship the greatness of our Lord. I really mean worship. That means meditate on, sing to, rejoice in, pray to, be thankful for *and* read about our great Lord. The Lord has given us all kinds of tools to enable us to do that, including Scripture, hymnbooks, theology books, and creation itself.

Your stubborn desires will only change by being replaced—through the power of the Holy Spirit—by superior desires. I believe that happens through worship. If false worship is the problem, true worship is the solution!

Why is it important to deal with your heart? Because dealing with your heart and its desires will help you to respond differently to your family, and that will breathe hope into a seemingly hopeless situation. Much more importantly, rooting out and replacing the false worship of your inner person will help you grow in Christlikeness. Paul David Tripp captures this idea precisely:

> *While we focus on good results, God focuses on the process of making us good. We judge his faithfulness on the basis of how many of our desires he has met. But his intent is to free us from our bondage to sinful desires.*[8]

Our Lord wants to use your pressured circumstances to help you get free from the false worship of your soul. As you work on changing the treasure of your heart, your character traits will change, and hope will be given to your spouse that your relationship could be different.

Practical Suggestions

To conclude this chapter, here are some practical suggestions for strengthening relationships in the midst of the intense pressure that comes from living with special needs.

Commit to a Church Family

One of the most important phrases in the New Testament is "one another." It captures the closeness that should be evident in relationships in a church. This is powerfully portrayed in Romans 12:

> So we, though many, are one body in Christ, and individually members *one of another*. . . . Let love be genuine. . . . Love *one another* with brotherly affection. Outdo *one another* in showing honor. . . .
> . . . Contribute to the needs of the saints and seek to show hospitality. . . . Live in harmony with *one another*. Do not be haughty, but associate with the lowly.
> (12:5, 9, 10, 13, 16)[9]

I was amazed and rejoiced when Tony and Jo Knott told me that 300 volunteers from church were helping them during the most intense times. This is a beautiful example of Galatians 6:2:

> *Bear one another's burden, and so fulfill the law of Christ.*

Do you have a good church family? If you are the primary caregiver for your spouse or child, do you have healthy relationships in your church?

If you need suggestions for how to find a good church, read Jim Newheiser's mini-book in this series, *Help! I Need a Church*.

Be a Team

Our Lord designed marriage to be a "one flesh" relationship. Through God's beautiful design we do not have to deal with the rough waters of life alone. Maybe this will take an attitude adjustment on your part. Are you an independent person who has a tendency to think you do not need others? Do you have to prove to others you are strong? If so, instead of wearing yourself out with your independence, accept that humans are made to be relational and not to go through life alone. Let your spouse be your teammate. Be a teammate for your spouse. What do you need to do to make that happen?

Trust God's Plans

God's Good Purposes

One of the many things I love about Scripture is how realistic it is. The promises of Scripture are set against the realities of brokenness. The stories of deliverance are about real people with immense problems, and about how God was faithful. Most often, though, his faithfulness is seen while they writhed in pain, both physical and relational. What did these people do? They chose to believe the promises of God in the midst of the turmoil; they struggled with their minds and their souls to believe truth. Psalm 18 is a perfect example of this.

If you are going to follow their example, you must believe that God is up to something good. He wastes no pain, and the cross is the prime example of that! Tony and Jo Knott write,

> *Rhonda was not a surprise to God, and He entrusted this child to us so that His love could be perfected through her life. [She] was here for a reason, and God used this precious child to bring strong men to their knees and helped lift up other parents with a disabled child with hope and purpose.*[10]

Back at the start of this mini-book, I told you about my friend John who is now paralyzed. Through the years I have been impressed with his faith. He has often told me that God has a purpose for all that has happened in his life.

Do you see what the Knotts and my friend are saying? Through the disability, God is accomplishing something beautiful in your life spiritually. Even though we are reluctant to accept it, Paul Tripp is correct when he writes,

> *God is creating eternal changes in my heart, and he will use trials and loss to accomplish this. His goal for me is not the abundance of earthly things, but the abundance of hope in God.*[11]

What you choose to believe in the midst of this intense, unexpected circumstance in your life will determine your success in stabilizing your marriage and handling the intensity of your situation. Jerry Bridges has captured well what it means to live trusting God:

> *Trust is not a passive state of mind. It is a vigorous act of the soul whereby we choose to lay hold on the promises of God and*

cling to them despite the adversity that at times seeks to overwhelm us.[12]

This is not easy. As Bridges says, it means you have to fight with your soul/mind to believe the promises of God right in the midst of trials. Your marriage will be much more stable if you live a life of trusting God. Instead of being tense, you can be at peace, which will lead to a calmer atmosphere in your home.

Walk with the Lord Together

It is important not only to trust the Lord, but to do so together. Are you and your spouse heading in the same direction spiritually? Are you praying together? Are you reading Scripture together? Please do not allow your hearts to withdraw from the Lord and from each other. It is too easy, in the midst of pressure, to grow cold spiritually. Fight against this and walk with the Lord together. Just as the Lord moved toward us with the gospel, so move toward one another and the Lord together.

Protect Your Sexual Relationship

You must protect not only your spiritual life, but also your physical intimacy. I know you are tired. I know it seems that every day is packed. To not do so, though, would be a violation of 1 Corinthians 7:

> *But because of the temptation to sexual immorality, each man should have his own wife and each woman her own husband. . . . Do not deprive one another, except perhaps by agreement for a* limited time, *that you may devote yourselves to prayer; but then come together again, so that Satan may not tempt you because of your lack of self-control.*
>
> (7:2, 5)

Communicate Frequently

When asked, "What has sustained your marriage while raising a child with a disability?" Jennifer responded by saying,

> *Throughout the last ten years of our marriage Michael and I [have] maintained consistent communication. We made each other a priority by spending time connecting spiritually, physically and emotionally. . . . We pray together and apart.*

Resolve Conflict

In a pressure-filled fallen world, conflict is inevitable, and leaving things unresolved is a natural tendency. But conflict must be resolved.

One resource the Lord has used to save thousands of marriages is Ken Sande's book *Peacemaking for Families*. I particularly recommend the guidelines it provides for how to work through difficult issues. Sande teaches an agenda to follow based upon Philippians 2:3–5.

Take Breaks

This ties in with the first suggestion above, of the importance of your church family. Whoever the main caregiver is needs regular breaks. And you and your spouse both need breaks together. This highlights the need for a good church family who will be willing to help you achieve this.

Conclusion

There is always hope when we know the Lord and seek to walk in the strength of his grace. That is what I have tried to communicate throughout this little book. A growing relationship with Jesus Christ as Lord and Savior makes healthy relationships with others possible, even when experiencing the pressure of disability. Because of who Jesus is, he can change or stabilize the climate in your home through the power of the gospel at work in your heart.

The testimonies from other couples who struggle with the same pressure show that it's possible to have closeness in marriage even while raising a child or caring for a spouse who has disabilities. This is possible because Jesus is reigning as Lord in their homes.

The following encouragement from Hebrews 12 is appropriate as we think of the different scenarios in which disability lives:

> *Therefore, since we are surrounded by so great a cloud of witnesses, let us also lay aside every weight, and sin which clings so closely, and let us run with endurance the race that is set before us, looking to Jesus, the founder and perfecter of our faith, who for the joy that was set before him endured the cross, despising the shame, and is seated at the right hand of the throne of God.*
>
> (12:1–2)

Having heard from other witnesses and having seen the example and power of Jesus, it is your turn to run the race. By the grace of God, you can do it!

Personal Application Projects

1. Think about the following character traits and evaluate yourself on a scale of 1–10: 1 = By the grace of God, I do not struggle with this at all; 5 = This is somewhat of a problem; 10 = I am weak in this area. Be brave. Then ask your spouse (or another person you trust) also to evaluate you.

- » Compassion (being tenderhearted toward others)
  - Spouse's evaluation
- » Kindness (doing nice things)
  - Spouse's evaluation
- » Humility (lowly minded, others-first mentality)
  - Spouse's evaluation
- » Meekness (gentle, under control)
  - Spouse's evaluation
- » Patience (not easily angered)
  - Spouse's evaluation
- » Bearing with one another (enduring with others)
  - Spouse's evaluation

- » Forgiveness (graciously giving to the undeserving)
  - Spouse's evaluation
- » Love (self-sacrificial giving of self for others)
  - Spouse's evaluation

2. Now evaluate yourself on the opposites, and again have your spouse (or another person you trust) give you an assessment as well: 1 = I do not struggle with this much; 5 = I kind of struggle with this; 10 = This is a big problem and is impacting our relationship.

- » Cold, hard-hearted, aloof (opposite of showing compassion)
  - Spouse's evaluation
- » Mean, maybe even cruel
  - Spouse's evaluation
- » Pride: life needs to be about you, a high view of your needs, expecting others to serve you
  - Spouse's evaluation
- » Rashness, snappy, harsh, a bully
  - Spouse's evaluation
- » Irritable, angry
  - Spouse's evaluation

» Intolerant, ready to give up, to let relationships wither
  - Spouse's evaluation

» Resentful, holding grudges, dwelling on offenses, desiring to punish
  - Spouse's evaluation

» Unloving, not serving others
  - Spouse's evaluation

3. Based upon your evaluation, which are your two weakest areas? Think of the situations in which these tendencies come out. Again, ask your spouse if you need help identifying this. Come up with a plan for how you will respond differently in those times.

4. What "treasures" (desires of your heart) feed these? In other words, work on identifying the false worship of your heart as revealed by your thinking, decision-making, emotions, and desires. All of these together reveal your deepest affections: the things you love, hope for, and place your faith in. Use the questions on the following pages to help you.

Mind

- What tends to occupy your mind?
- What tends to occupy your mind about your marriage?
- What tends to occupy your mind in relation to your family member's disability?

Will (decision-making)

- What do you tend to "protect"?
- If and when you have some free time, how do you choose to spend it?
- If you have any extra money, how do you choose to spend it?

Emotions

- What emotion is your biggest struggle right now? What does this reveal about the desires of your heart?
- When do you tend to struggle with fear or worry?
- What situations in life tend to stir up anger?

Desires

» What do you want that you are not getting?

» What are you getting that you do not want?

» What do you find yourself yearning for?

5. Having worked through question 4, what would you say is the ruling desire that feeds and provokes the opposites of the Christlike character traits? Remember that if you can identify it, you will be better able to come up with a biblical plan of what the opposite is, in order to attack it.

6. Having identified that wrong ruling desire in question 5, what is the opposite of it, biblically? What passages of Scripture help you think about how to attack these desires of your heart? Remember: if false worship is the problem, true worship is the solution. Here are some places to start:

» Controlling others: Isaiah 40–48

» Pleasing people: Proverbs 29:25

» Loving comfort: 2 Corinthians 1:3–12; Psalm 18:1–3

7. Do you have a church where you and your spouse are members, a place where you feel you are at home, and a church family you can rely on when things are hard? If you need help finding such a church, consult Jim Newheiser's mini-book, *Help! I Need a Church*.

8. Many of the psalms are laments. Two of my favorites are Psalms 42 and 43. Read these psalms out loud two or three times and then pray them back to the Lord, inserting your situation into the verses. This practice will help you express your own lament to the Lord.

9. Memorize the following definition of trust by Jerry Bridges and then pick two or three promises of God from Scripture that you will also commit to memory and choose to believe when tempted to despair or doubt:

> *Trust is not a passive state of mind. It is a vigorous act of the soul whereby we choose to lay hold on the promises of God and cling to them despite the adversity that at times seeks to overwhelm us.*[13]

Where Can I Get More Help?

Baker, Ernie, *Help! I'm in a Conflict* (Wapwallopen, PA: Shepherd Press, 2016).

Bridges, Jerry, *Trusting God, Even When Life Hurts* (Colorado Springs, CO: NavPress, 2017).

De Courcy, Philip, *Help! I'm Anxious* (Wapwallopen, PA: Shepherd Press, 2018).

Deuel, Dave, *Help! My Grandchild Has a Disability* (Wapwallopen, PA: Shepherd Press, 2019).

Eareckson Tada, Joni, and Steve Estes, *When God Weeps: Why Our Sufferings Matter to the Almighty* (Grand Rapids: Zondervan, 1997).

Harvey, Dave, *When Sinners "Say I Do"* (Wapwallopen, PA: Shepherd Press, 2007).

James, Joel, *Help! I Can't Handle All These Trials* (Wapwallopen, PA: Shepherd Press, 2014).

Knott, Jo, *Wake Up Rhonda: How a Courageous Family Rescued Their "Sleeping Beauty" from Severe Brain-Damage* (Jacksonville, FL: Brut Printing Company, 2015 update).

Newheiser, Jim, *Help! I Need A Church* (Wapwallopen, PA: Shepherd Press, 2016).

Peace, Martha, *The Excellent Wife* (Bemidji, MN: Focus, 1995).

Sande, Ken, *Peacemaking for Families* (Ada, MI: Baker, 2002).

Scott, Stuart, *The Exemplary Husband* (Bemidji, MN: Focus, 2000).

Tripp, Paul David, *Suffering: Eternity Makes a Difference* (Phillipsburg, NJ: P&R, 2001).

Endnotes

1 Jo Knott, *Wake Up Rhonda!* (Jacksonville, FL: Brut Printing Company, 2015), 24, 27.

2 Andrew and Rachel, private correspondence, July 18, 2018. Their names and details, as well as those of several other persons mentioned in this book, have been changed to protect their privacy.

3 Tony and Jo Knott, private correspondence, July 14, 2018.

4 The connection between the two books is demonstrated through the same people being referred to in both.

5 All definitions are from William Arndt and F. Wilbur Gingrich, *A Greek–English Lexicon of the New Testament* (Grand Rapids: Zondervan, 1963).

6 "Worship," at www.thefreedictionary.com: "from Old English weorthscipe : weorth, worth; + -scipe, -ship." Accessed March 15, 2013.

7 LORD (with small capitals) is being used here in the Old Testament sense of the one true living God as contrasted with idols.

8 Paul David Tripp, *Suffering: Eternity Makes a Difference* (Phillipsburg, NJ: P&R, 2001), 16.

9 All emphasis in Scripture quotes in this mini-book has been added.

10 Knott, private correspondence.

11 Tripp, *Suffering*, 9.

12 Jerry Bridges, *Trusting God, Even When Life Hurts* (Colorado Springs, CO: NavPress, 2008), 202.

13 Bridges, *Trusting God*, 202.

joni&friends

It is our great pleasure at Joni & Friends International Disability Center to endorse this mini-book, *Help! Disability Pressures Our Marriage*, produced by Shepherd Press. We pray this resource will bless you in your journey.

Joni & Friends is answering the call in the Gospel of Luke, chapter 14, "invite the poor, the crippled, the lame, the blind, and you will be blessed.... make them come in so my house will be full." Our mission at Joni & Friends is to communicate the gospel and equip Christ-honoring churches worldwide to evangelize and disciple people affected by disabilities.

We present the gospel of Jesus Christ to all people affected by disability and their families who are served through our programs around the world. We train, disciple, and mentor people affected by disability to exercise their gifts of leadership and service in their churches and communities. Visit us at https://www.joniandfriends.org/ministries/ to learn about all our ministries, such as Wheels for the World, Family Retreats, and radio and television ministries, and to find an area ministry office near you.

Contact Joni & Friends

- Visit our website, www.joniandfriends.org.
- For help and inspiration, visit https://www.joniandfriends.org/help-inspiration/.
- To find out how you can get involved, visit https://www.joniandfriends.org/support-us/.

Books in the Help! series include...

Help! He's Struggling with Pornography
Help! Someone I Love Has Been Abused
Help! My Toddler Rules the House
Help! Someone I Love Has Cancer
Help! I Want to Change
Help! My Spouse Has Been Unfaithful
Help! Someone I Love Has Alzheimer's
Help! I Have Breast Cancer
Help! I'm a Slave to Food
Help! My Teen Struggles With Same-Sex Attractions
Help! She's Struggling With Pornography
Help! I Can't Get Motivated
Help! I'm a Single Mom
Help! I'm Confused About Dating
Help! I'm In a Painful Marriage
Help! My Grandchild Has a Disability
Help! I'm Drowning in Debt
Help! My Teen is Rebellious
Help! I'm Depressed
Help! I'm Living With Terminal Illness
Help! I Feel Ashamed
Help! I Want to Model Submission in Marriage
Help! I Can't Handle All These Trials
Help! I Can't Forgive
Help! My Anger is Out of Control
Help! My Friend is Suicidal
Help! I'm in a Conflict
Help! I'm Being Deployed
Help! I've Been Traumatized by Combat
Help! I'm So Lonely
Help! My Kids Are Viewing Pornography
Help! I Need a Church
Help! I'm Anxious
Help! My Parents Abused Me When I was a Kid

More titles in preparation

For current listing go to: www.shepherdpress.com/lifeline